RAW

RAW

An Asian American Narrative

Natalie Y. Ahn

RAW
AN ASIAN AMERICAN NARRATIVE

iUniverse books may be ordered through booksellers or by contacting:

iUniverse
1663 Liberty Drive
Bloomington, IN 47403
www.iuniverse.com
844-349-9409

Because of the dynamic nature of the Internet, any web addresses or
links contained in this book may have changed since publication and
may no longer be valid. The views expressed in this work are solely those
of the author and do not necessarily reflect the views of the publisher,
and the publisher hereby disclaims any responsibility for them.

Any people depicted in stock imagery provided by Getty Images are
models, and such images are being used for illustrative purposes only.
Certain stock imagery © Getty Images.

ISBN: 978-1-6632-2392-0 (sc)
ISBN: 978-1-6632-2391-3 (e)

Library of Congress Control Number: 2021919155

Print information available on the last page.

iUniverse rev. date: 11/19/2021

For all the special people in my life who have made this journey possible—I love you for who you once were, for all you are now, and for all you will come to be.

RAW

Naked

Vulnerable

Unadulterated

Bloody

Toxic

Lethal

Stripped down.

This is what life has come to.

Preface

Here Is My Beginning,

Head down, sunglasses and mask on, baseball cap pulled low, I grabbed what was on the grocery list from my mother as quickly as possible. My father's voice echoed in my mind as I sped through the produce section. *Don't stay longer than you have to.*

The first wave of the pandemic back in March 2020 brought Asian xenophobia into full throttle. Even in my small Caucasian town, I was noticing strange interactions. Whether it was the disapproving shake of a head or a full-on racial slur, it incited fear in me I couldn't shake. And this proved to be difficult to ignore when I was consistently the only Asian person in the room. I was a child again—kids were stretching their eyes sideways at me, singing *ching chong* in accented voices, laughing at the food I brought for lunch. I was "ugly"; "smelly"; and, worse, an outsider.

In seventh grade, I was assigned a family tree presentation. I interviewed my grandmother and grew excited over the stories she told about our family, who created a soybean milk company to get protein to lactose-intolerant children, reforested the Korean Peninsula after the war, and built schools. I stayed up perfecting my poster, carefully cutting and pasting pictures, and ironing my traditional Korean *hanbok*. For the first time, I was excited to talk about my family.

But the other presentations were about white families on big Southern porches with family crests embossed onto their giant door knockers. I felt silly next to those photos in my dress. My ears started ringing and cheeks started to burn. The colors suddenly looked gaudy and childish; the rainbow sleeves too loud—not at all like the intricate silk tapestry I had spent hours ironing the night before. I took off my jade headpiece and stuffed it into my bag.

I presented as quickly as possible, rushing through the details, leaving out my favorite parts to just get it over with. My shame rushed back—my three-generation household, missing out on "normal" weekends because of Saturday Korean school, my slanted eyes, my grandmother's inability to speak English. I wanted so badly to be the same as everybody else.

So I taped my eyes so they would appear larger, dyed my hair, and changed what I wore. I stopped attending Korean school and bought cafeteria lunches. I made the friends I longed for but still felt out of place. No matter how much I changed, I was never quite "right" enough to slide into place and fit in. Chronically inadequate—a feeling that no amount of flavored lip gloss could fix. I was still the little girl who was too afraid to eat her lunch in front of her classmates.

This estrangement followed me to boarding school, where I was shunned by Asians for being "too white" and rejected by Caucasians because I wasn't. Some of the other girls in my freshman dorm had dubbed me a "rich, white, suburban girl." Even though I had been trying to be the girl they described for my whole life, their words still stung in a way that left me stunned. My self-loathing only amplified when I faced rejection because I didn't fit into the singular definitions of "white" or "Asian." I was both and neither, which meant I didn't belong anywhere. I didn't rediscover my identity or gain self-confidence until I was around sixteen.

But part of this newfound self-confidence was rooted in the fetishization of Asian women, because it felt like I had become desirable overnight. I had grown out of my lanky awkwardness and crossed the fine line between "girl" and "woman," simultaneously painting a target symbolizing adulthood on my back. "Rich, white, suburban girl" was quickly replaced by "exotically beautiful," and being so starved for recognition, I took whatever I could. People told me I should be flattered, so I was. When you've been an outcast your whole life, being not only acceptable but also coveted feels like an insane victory. The concepts of deeply engrained racism and fetishization never crossed my mind. I still feel bad for the girl who thought that burying her shame would work if she lost herself with it.

It is easy to believe what you're told as a kid, especially when you've been waiting to hear it all your life. Then why did I somehow know, deep down, it wasn't really me being accepted, just my potential to fulfill a stereotype?

I was only able to truly confront my racial shame when I was able to look in the mirror and not see someone who was so painfully different or derive worth from being a sexual preference. The comments surrounding Asian stereotypes that were so ingrained in student culture started to slide off more easily. My skin grew into Teflon, and soon, nothing that used to bother me could stick. The more years that passed, the more unapologetic I became. I had found the only truth I needed inside the walls of my house and in my family history, and I wasn't going to suppress it out of fear any longer.

Come March 2020, the self-acceptance I had nurtured since high school was cancelled out by fear. The eyes, hair, and body I had grown proud of became identifiers that were used against me. I was in middle school again, standing in a sea of blond hair.

Still, I kept up with current events. Korean faces were on the front lines of the pandemic, searching for a cure. I watched their case numbers drop as they gained better control and understanding of the virus and became the model for handling Covid. Thousands of miles away, my heart swelled for the country fighting for the future amid the racial tension and violence that petrified me.

I remember how insignificant and disempowered I had felt all my life. I recall the shaking in my voice and ringing in my ears during my family tree presentation. How could I ever forget the stinging in my eyes from holding back tears while people made fun of me on the school bus "behind my back"? Or when random people started to message me on social media, saying that "they had never been with an Asian girl before"? How could I forget trying to learn to live while experiencing perpetual disgust and fear? It was time to stop acting as if I had done something wrong.

The fear didn't dissipate overnight and is long from gone, but I made slow progress. I can leave the house without hiding my face and trying to melt into the background. People's second glances no longer make my stomach churn. I stopped making an active effort to be invisible but, rather, aim to be impossible to miss.

I'm not a statistic, an outsider, or predisposed to be a victim of violence. The unnerving state of the world is not an excuse for regression. I should never shrink away from adversity or diminish myself out of fear. It is time to stop hiding what makes me feel special. It is time to stop snuffing out my words because they make other people "uncomfortable." It is time we emerge into the world unafraid, ready, and willing to fight.

I am a part of the Ahn family. I am proud. That is more than enough.

This is me finding my voice.

2020

we are emboldened by risk and held together with love.

at least i think that is what we should be;

anything can be dangerous when in possession of the wrong person.

swans in glass jars

A man raised a baby swan in a glass jar, but as the bird grew
it became stuck in the jar. The man was caught now, for the
only way to free the thing was to break the jar, killing the swan.

—Zen saying from *The Book of Awakening*
by Mark Nepo

as feathers push against glass, you wonder why it never occurred
to you that the tiny wet delicate being you held in your claws
would grow too large to make that jar its home.

was it ignorance? or simply lack of forethought? because
you were busy at the time, so much so that this insignificant
hatchling was inconsequential to the grand scheme of your
cinematic life.

you sat on your throne with a haughty grin because you, being
the benevolent ruler you are, were kind enough to give this
pitiful repulsive thing a home and your protection.

and when you hear its strangled screams, you realize that you never meant for your conceited fraudulence to ruin something that could grow to be graceful; you never looked past the ugly.

now you have a decision to make: kill it or it will kill itself.

Homesick

Smoky nights and fireplace warmed
This is the site of my every victory and demise.
Not remembering what I saw through my opalescent windows,
Groveling nightly at the foot of the stairs,
Elation undulating through the air each morning.
Languishing without my mother's laundry detergent
Lamenting leaping from the nest before I had grown into my
wings.

Life goes flat, so I stay in bed.
My fear is staccato
My pain vibrato
It goes sharp and I wail instead.
My home is where my heart is.

I am waiting for something and nothing
A malignant abyss scratching its way inside.
This world has antagonized the undercurrent of my ignorance,
Disturbing the balance I once found absolute.
A curt goodbye is all I was able to get
Before being forced to jump ship

The saline I am swimming in stings,
But at least my tears will have friends.

I regret the time I was callous and proud
To go back to change my mind,
To stay hopeful and be kind;
Perhaps I could be rid of this dismal shroud.
My home is where my heart is.

Love

I'm from late-night movies and home-cooked meals
Grapefruit perfume and oud cologne
I'm from a patchwork fence at the corner of a pond
The same pond that overflows when it rains
I'm from a one-stoplight town with frequent power outages
Topped off with air-popped corn kernels slathered in butter

I am my mother's heart, my father's brain;
I am her voice and his student
I am my brother's tears;
He wept more for me than he did himself
I am my grandmother's hands;
Every detail carefully crafted with love

I became my sweet intentions and marshmallow skies
I am fragrant early light and the swell of the wind
I am nails bitten down to the beds of calloused fingertips
I am the hearth that adores me and brain that guides me
I am the tears that remind me and the safety net underneath
I am all these things; I am my family; I am bulletproof

DO WE FEEL THE SAME FEAR?

i see girls like me and men like my father afraid to leave the house

knifed in the aisles of grocery stores, spat on in the streets

heckled on daily walks without a trace of remorse from the perpetrator and yet

men and women who look like me serve on the front lines leading research to a cure,

working daylong shifts and risking their lives only to change out of scrubs and walk onto the street and return to the life of an Asian person during a global pandemic:

> *Chink.*
> *China virus.*
> *This is your fault.*
> *Go back to where you came from.*

my country fares well today because of its tragic history—

conquered occupied oppressed raped pillaged killed nearly wiped out so we hold each other close in a time where we again are being marginalized, but yet we are still

the ones giving new technology, providing medications, offering help and for what?

to be spat on and to have our children stabbed by people incensed with an unfounded hatred,

targeted for what others have done but are you not human as well?

are you not to share equally in this blame

are you not acting as a villain in this story by targeting people who have done nothing more than you?

we are the same people who wish to live to see the same things;

we dream the same dreams and bleed the same red.

i am not your scapegoat.

A Day with Me

At 5:00 a.m., blink out the dark
Get out of bed only to go back to sleep
Wake up with the climax of the sun at daybreak
Let your stomach drop through your toes
Drag yourself across the floor until you are the last one awake
Do this every day

Your hands are weak; allow them to tremble
Toss your pebbled wishes into the pond;
Watch ripples spread in glassy charcoal
Let the bugs bite; do not itch
Pollen falls across your nose like yellow freckles
Your eyes will water; let it drip down

I despise the morning and detest the night
I delight in the solitude when time stands still,
The sole sound being my heartbeat;
Or maybe it's yours.
In limbo where it is neither today nor yesterday nor tomorrow,
The stars are barely there; so am I

Do you feel the sharpness in your sternum
The ache underneath your eyes, raw, red,
Neck scorched with every touch

Do you feel the prison that is your body
Are you aware of every part of it that has not yet
Felt the time of day that stands still

Are you in pain

Dear Heart

Dear heart that makes its home in my chest,
The one that longs to nestle close to yours,
Tissue paper wings fluttering with every rise and fall
Please do not tear your stitches out.

Dear heart that fills the space between my ears with thoughts
of you,
The itch cannot be scratched; the feeling will not fade.
If you are a shadow, you will be my shadow.
I will take you as you are.

Dear heart that disintegrates at every turn,
Your layers peel off like a ripe orange
Ready to be plucked and sucked
By any mouth that wishes to have a taste.

Dear heart that lies alone in my bed
Forlorn and beguiling,
A gushing core is still beneath the flaking crust;
The stronghold will only cradle you for so long.

Letters to Loved Ones

To everyone I love, you have my gratitude.
I can be a difficult person to be around;
Enough to where even I can't keep up
With the flashing images that pass us by.
I would like to contextualize myself
So maybe you will understand me a little bit more.

1.
I live on an orange pine needle carpet and purple flowers in
the spring,
Circular driveways, and smooth roads paid with tax dollars,
White picket fences and colonial houses,
Snow every winter,
A roaring fire,
That is my home.

I come from chicken wire science projects,
Play-Doh and Legos,
And long-distance dreams of a world that seemed so far away
at the age of eight
but was much closer than I thought
And not at all as nice as I had wished for.

I come from one element in two worlds, straddling divides between universes,
Whiffs of fresh-baked cookies and pickled radish.
I come from semiannual visits to the dentist and braces on and off twice before I was thirteen.
I come from love.
I also come from the hardship that lives behind the white picket fences around the colonial houses.

I come from angry bedtimes and teary mornings,
Puffy eyes and swollen lips.
I come from screaming matches that take place in my head
And holes in our perfectly paved roads that only I can see.

I have fallen into the craters enough times that
the wet cement has molded to fit my form.
And this is what I call home.

2.

To everyone I loved—

Thank you.

There are days when I lament over your loss.

There are weeks when I feel like a day without you is a day without the sun.

There are months where your idling fabrications were my suffocation,

But that could be the Irish Spring soap in your shower.

There are times when I only listen to songs that remind me of you,

The ones we used to sing in the car.

Jon Secada sang your first breakup song.

"It's just another day without you."

That is all today is,

And that is all tomorrow with be.

Thank you for teaching me how to go a day without sun.

3.

To everyone I don't love anymore,

This is my public apology, though most of you will never hear it
Because my pride rides too high on my shoulders to let the
words spill out of my mouth.

I still love you even though I claim that that part of me is dead.

Your leaving took a part out of me as well,

The part that uttered the words, "I love you."

I fell in love with something there, but that something
disappeared after a while.

Let me know if it resurfaces.

Yearning

I sit by the window and wait,

Legs tensed, nails tapping,

Watching every molecule of air brushing the trees,

Waiting for a day when time does not drag by quite so slow.

I wait for you to appear,

An apparition on the mesh screen.

I bide my time for the day you do not wait

To come out after we are cloaked in a blanket of midnight blue.

I pine for the day, the hour, minute, second
Where you stand before me,
No longer only a wish,
No longer a phantom body or figment of imagination.

I prepare for when you are more than a scintillating dream,
When your skin is warm to the touch,
The dulcet tinkle of your laugh
Radiating luminosity

When I can see an iridescent soul lift above your head,
Float up among the clouds
To watch you dance intertwined in layers of chiffon
Billowing around my waist until you disappear from sight.

I admit this desire to be ridden with guilt,
For the time I lost that was not with you,
When you could not be loved in the way you deserve,
When you could not love me in the ways I needed.

But how I wait,

Yearning

For the day of our redemption to come.

Glass People

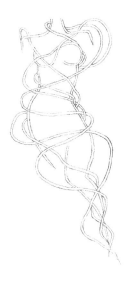

Each day I bandage every inch of my body,
Layered cotton so thick that I cannot feel the touch of a stranger,
A measure of prevention to not break in transit
Or in the grasp of a careless fool.
Today everyone seems that way.

I am wrapped to double my size
To provide a cushion because at the moment,
Feeling nothing is better than being fractured;

Sacrificing your touch is a small price to pay—
A poignant thought considering that is all I long for.

I have not run my palms over your glossy constitution
I still find myself tantalized by your skin,
Only my eyes are left uncovered
To watch glass people shatter each other,
Remorseless, thoughtless, unfeeling.

Hearing you hit the floor is sonorous—
Rain hitting a skylight, a breaking pane beneath my fist
Left cracked; forgotten
We walk to have pieces of you stick into our feet.
The scar tissue grows thick on our soles.

United We stand, divided We fall

today, we do not stand together.
i can barely see you from where i am
you are a paltry speck standing against a paper cutout backdrop.
you do not matter when you are alone.

your chants rise up into the sky and rest among the clouds
along with the rest of the unheard cries,
with the maltreated, the slandered.
no one is tall enough to poke a hole in the atmosphere to free us.

united We stand; divided We fall.
today begins the age of descent.

a hand for holding

i wish someone would tell me that they should have been there to catch me i wish i knew that there were people in the world who would snap to attention when the bomb drops but instead i am leaving a trail of breadcrumbs away from the dead bodies that pile up every time we are ignored every time someone tells me that it was not a *hate crime* there was no motive we are not in danger we have nothing to be afraid of we are not people of color we are the model minority we are supposed to be quiet but how can i let the world choke the air out of me when i have so much to say i will not be crushed i refuse to be crushed i refuse to be ignored.

The Perfect Game

The machination you believe will lead to my vanquishment:

Powder me to put in the rain and watch me melt
Peel back my hide to see if I am truly flesh and blood
Overturn every cell to ensure you are not being deceived

Hack open my ribcage to release a crimson fountain
Take inventory of all inactive elements that dwell within
Let me leave a trail of red on the floor

If it takes slicing me from top to bottom to prove
That I am no different than you,
Then it must be; my name must be written on the moon

It will not blow away.
I will not melt.
I will not cede to you.

Bottle my blood; obliterate my likeness
No matter how relentless,
You will never sincerely succeed

I am a chess piece in this perfect game,
The rulebook written by the curve of my lip,
Made of marble but not the queen

You are playing on my board,
Harvesting my work,
Eating out of my hand.

I will be the perpetual champion
Regardless of your attempts to bend the rules,
You will never rupture the bubble of my tranquil fervor.

And yet
You are still intent
On winning my perfect game.

hope

hope is different from delusion and i would like someone anyone to come out with a message that does not mix both "the truth" does not mean much anymore.

Let's Be Beautiful

Happiness,
An elusive concept:
Defined as "the state of feeling happy."

Is it the elation of hearing you love me?
or that I know it without having to hear a word
Soft footfalls and forehead kisses

Is it the best meal you've ever tasted?
Warm flavor rolling across taste buds,
Sour sugar melting to numb cheeks.

"Happy" is too soapy to cling to.
"Happy" is difficult to fathom.
"Happy" slips away every time you forget exactly what "happy" is.

Let's be beautiful instead;
Let us lay in the grass to be broiled by stars,
To be bathed in dappled sunlight until we are engulfed in gold.

Let us be beautiful; let us be happy.
Let us be made of pulsing light and refracted beams
Until beautiful and happy are one and the same.

It is hard to stay happy; it is easy to stay beautiful.

Let us have a penchant for our morning breath and sleepy days.
Let us gaze upon our likeness with upturned mouths in return.

Let me run until there is a hammer threatening to breach my lungs
And let the glittering pieces fall.
For as long as we are happy, we are beautiful.

Cry for Me

I watch the ripples spread across the holes I bored into your face,

A telltale sign you're going to cry.

You don't have to lie to me anymore,

I see my reflection in those tarnished eyes.

That is all the truth I need to go on.

Freezer Burn

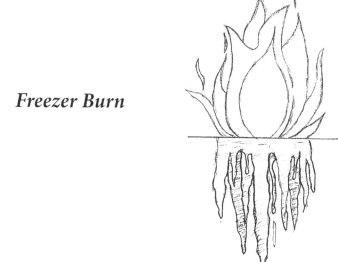

there is no place that is as cold as you.

we were never taught that fire is not the only thing that burns

keep your child away from matches; but the ice cubes from the freezer are fine

when i felt you go frigid i was not afraid but should have been.

i left my extremities in the subzero for 2 years too long, milky white freezer burn creeping spidering

into the heart you left cold but there will still never be a place that is as cold as you.

seventytwo hours

"bittersweet" is the souring aftertaste of coffee that lingers on my tongue long after you are gone and the staticky black-and-white cogitation you left behind.

Red Roads

the roads I used to trace back you were sunburned
brickish and faded, like someone had wiped off their leftover
paint

when I miss you I slit my palms and drag them through my town
the hope being that maybe, just maybe, you might follow the
red roads back to me

but you don't know about the red roads, or my drying blood on
the asphalt of my neighborhood
the sun bakes it until it rusts and withers; how am I without you

The Gallows

embark on this journey with me.
i did not perish from asphyxiation
but from the burnished demons lurking
around the bend of the path.

beware; they will captivate you
using cloying words, syrupy adulations
underneath an angelic disguise.
perhaps, like me, you have encountered them before.

join me in the hallowed scaffolds.
your life has been curtailed as well.
may we swing in rapture of all those recalled,
our sighs becoming a fervent lullaby.

how silly it is that we looked for solace in roseate complexions,
intoxicated by the heady aroma of bleach,
crucified by confiture,
undaunted by the temper boiling beneath the surface.

Vows

I

Take thee, you

Who takes the world by storm,

Single-handedly adorning the walls of my heart,

To be my forever, everlasting,

To have and to hold from this day forward,

For better, drunk with ecstasy,

For worse, drenched in sorrow,

For richer with life,

For poorer than poverty-stricken and starved,

In sickness of the world

And in health of our country,

To love and to cherish

As we do our freedom,

Till death do us part,

To be your eternal lifeline,

Until some power may come between us.

I pledge thee my faith,

My loyalty, my devotion, my everlasting love.

Fragments

Maybe if I could freeze you in time
then you would stop hurting me.

We would be empty husks of humans,
desiccated, wilting, wizened.

But your hair was soft and your smile was sweet,
and that was all it took.

When looking at myself, all I see
is where you touched me,
hurt me.
But it all looks the same.

So what does it mean for me now
if one can't differentiate between fear and love?

Fountain Pens

I smudged the end of our story—
We aren't at our expiration date quite yet.

Citizenship

"You shall love your neighbor as you love yourself"
(Mark 12:31).

Or

The position or status of being a citizen of a particular country.

1.

The slip of paper granting you access across a singular line

Into a new realm of life full of possibilities,

The American dream

Or the American nightmare,

Of which you cannot tell yet.

But hope pulses in every word spoken in a native tongue

Of people flowing through the gates to a new beginning.

2.

We are a labyrinth of jumbled twine,

Our relationships knots; love, tangles.

When one endeavors to extricate our mess,

We become loose in their fingers, and all resilience in our fibers

crumbles.

There are some snags that cannot be undone,
Blind to our pleas for liberation.
The knot grows tighter still until the pain crescendos enough
Your brain stops the feeling altogether.

3.

There are times that fluctuate with the drop of a pin
And times that are malleable like the change in the wind.
There are times when you need to be held to feel safe,
When times come and times go; we will all need a place
To hide and to hurt, to fall up or down, an escape from this
hauntingly lonely town.
We tie our belts tighter and hold ourselves higher
Above rushing water, a few feet from the ground.
You can't tie rocks to your ankles and expect not to drown.
The knots are all tied, the deals have been sealed,
The citizens of your heart, your sword and your shield.
When time draws to a close and ash turns to glitter,
Hang on to the sweet and remember the bitter;

Remember the cold and how the sun sets at four,
Cherish the love and what lies in store.
These people all back you as time has shown,
A citizen in our hearts, and never alone.

4.
i am the city of lights, but there are two.
i am pastel K-pop and the concrete jungle,
seoul or New York City; you cannot tell the difference.
i am a stereotype.
my legs only stretch so far over the gap
bridging over two continents, two cities, two lives.
i am confusing because i do not fit into either.
the city of lights?
i belong to both.

being from a different country does not make me
insignificant or evil or lazy; rather, i find that i am quite

passionate about who and what i love and will always

overcome the obstacles you place before me so, when a mother

cries for the death of her child, know that i was not culpable.

always watching my back i am

afraid of what will happen when i am not looking because

people i do not know wish me harm, and

i hope that my family will not cry for me.

Dear World,

I am so angry. I am unforgivably disheartened and broken. I am losing faith in you and everything good I once thought we stood for. I am scared. I am petrified. I feel alone in my anticipatory grief waiting for the shot in the dark you sent for me to lodge in my ribs. If I could single-handedly punch through the ozone layer and let the vacuum of space suck us dry, I would, because that would be better than your creations turning on each other the way they are now.

Dear World, be better for me my family, my children. You know we can do better. We have to be better. If there is a light at the end of the tunnel, give us a sign; if you have any power, inject the hateful with kindness. Please help to bring us contentment.

Dear World, you gave humanity the opportunity to choose good or evil and claim that you will love us either way. But I do not love the others. If that is a sin, then why give us the choice?

Dear Humanity, choosing to be evil is significantly easier than choosing to be good. I did not lie when I said I would love all my creations regardless. There is a light at the end of the tunnel; if you want reach it, you must be kind. The lost are the hardest to love.

Falling down the Rabbit Hole

My love, I am falling down again,
My love, I am slipping down the drain,
My love, I am afraid this time I have failed,
You cannot fix what is broken; the ship has set sail.

Your arms were open, so down I fell,
My only wish tossed into the well,
I tumbled down with it with a push from behind,
With an aged rotting heart growing benign.

I followed your trail too closely before,
Though I still am unsure as to what it is for,
When you keep getting shot, you'd think that you'd run,
But the game you're playing is all too much fun.

Who was that stranger who paid the toll,
Shredding my dignity then trying to console,
Whatever life I had left to have and to hold,
When you pulled me down the rabbit hole.

Masterpiece

I was blanker than a stark white canvas.
Under a microscope,
Waxy fibers weave back and forth,
Stretched over a wooden frame,
Waiting to be showered with color and turned
Into every sentiment belonging to me.

Only when I closed my eyes
Could I see my future
And in my outstretched fingers was you.

Standing as still as I was blank,
Armed with a soul filled with colors and subconscious filled
with fantasy,
Waiting for me to turn into your masterpiece.

Only when I close my eyes
Do I become the paint spread beneath your fingers,
The clay stuck underneath your nails,
Tactile enough to hold
The blues of your azure skies
And the oranges of your melting afternoons.

Only when I closed my eyes
Shaded from sight
And the curvature of the earth,
Disappeared with my vision
Was I a sight to behold,
Suspended in time.

Only when I closed my eyes did I feel like your masterpiece.
When they finally opened again

I see what you had done to me
The blood on your hands and dirt under your nails.
You had killed whatever beauty I thought I held,
But I was your masterpiece.

Or so I felt when shielded from the rest of the world;
When I closed my eyes and expected to feel you,
I was met with the bitter cold of metal pressed against my mouth,
Sealing me inside the fibers of the canvas,
You turned me into a masterpiece—
Your timeless, artistic emotional turmoil.

Down in a hole filled with your contusions, welded shut.
I can still feel your color flickering,
Tattooed to me,
Seeping into my pores,
Euphoria whistling through the air.
And I feel like a masterpiece again.

Pretty Girls Don't Cry

When I cry, there are streams of inky makeup that trail down
my cheeks.
They stain rivers down my neck and dry
Into thick, salty ribbons
But you're stroking my face,
Telling me, "Pretty girls don't cry."

I don't feel like a pretty girl,
Not when I'm alone
Looking at my misery,
With thick, salty, black ribbons wrapped around my neck,
Tightening with every palpitation.

With each hiccupped gasp, I see your eyes
Telling me, "Pretty girls don't cry."

I don't feel like a pretty girl until I feel you in my closet,
Breath coursing through bloodstreams,
I want to melt into you and dissipate all at once.

And I ask myself if that would be such a bad thing at all.
Losing the game was breaking in half,
With the only trace left of your voice telling me
Pretty girls don't cry.
I don't feel pretty, and I don't want to cry.

Sometimes if I sit in the dark for too long, I envision you,
Of how you have your mother's hands
And the way they snipped the black ribbons around my neck
When you told me
Pretty girls don't cry.

Battleground

in Korean tradition,
i am supposed to sit
back straight, ankles crossed
in a dress made from silk threads extracted from the colors of
heaven,
a red ribbon
tied around the end of one long braid
to signal that i am young,
unmarried, untainted,
innocent, pure, untouched.
a child,
ridiculed for slouching,
for the uneven curve of my fingers balanced above piano keys,
for ankles not crossed, for thighs not touching,
for not acting like a lady or being perceived as attractive,
for talking too much,
for being lanky and awkward.
my body became a battleground for others to intrude,
to fight, explore.
the red ribbons in my hair and straight spine make me more
doll,
less human.

poised smiles and pinched cheeks were supposed to make me plastic,
perfect, coveted, desirable.
ugly tears made me too slippery to hold onto.
it seems that people believe it is much easier
to hold a Barbie than an evolving concept,
to take a straight-shooting highway instead of a back road.
the view is obsolete.
plastic brains can't make chemical engineers.
airbrushed eyes cannot breathe oceans.
my hot-blooded complexion does not make me defective.
my condolences if you prefer polymer to pores.
your doll box will be my casket;
make up my face and display over my wintry rigid figure,
that is the only way you will obtain my compliance.

DOLLS OF THE WORLD
- SOUTH KOREA -

THE #1 MANUFACTURER OF TRADITIONALLY PERFECT GIRLS!

Would You Like That Gift Wrapped?

i would be your perfect present,
tied up with all the threads and trappings,
wrapped in the paper of your favorite colors.
everything about this box is alluring,
the perfect weight in your hand,
the most pleasing color to tickle your irises,
the softest touch and most decadent sound.
i give you my permission to open-
be wary.
attempts to unravel the twine will leave your fingertips minced.
ripping the paper will leave cuts across your palms.
opening will release crushing weight into your sternum,
brimming with guilt when you decide to drop it.
so you may open me,
but be wary.
years of perfecting the outside have made my insides turn to
sludge.

the illusion is completed with a perfect life,
a pretty face
in the nicest gift wrapping we have available!
so go ahead and open me
bear in mind the outside is much more palatable,
and that we don't accept gift receipts.

Heroes & Villains

Villains are not green-skinned people dressed in black
Nor are they the sanguine monsters that hide beneath our beds.
They are the skeletons in our closets,
The dark thoughts that flit through your subliminal storyline,
The impulse to leave everyone else behind; for they are just
dead weight.

We wish to be heroes, but we are villains who occasionally do
some good.
I am the bad guy in my own story.
I am the reason I am held back; I am the person who gets in
my way.
I am the one who makes bad choices, who makes mistakes,
The one who is lazy, who chooses herself above others, lies, sins.
I am the villain; I am the monster underneath the bed.

"Heroes" do not truly exist
There is no one to rescue you
Your protagonist has no superpowers
There is only us;
It is only us.

We are the people who take care of our loved ones
We are the people who strive to do good

I am no hero, but I attempt to do something small but good
Perhaps changing the world in one microscopic way is better
than not changing it at all.
I am not a villain who wishes ill on others,
Killing, looting, causing mass panic to "make a point."
I am not a hero,
I do not put out fires or save lives.

I am neither a hero nor a villain,
Simply a person who tries to do good
because changing the world in one small way
is better than being complacent in watching it burn.

Catharsis

there is something stuck in my throat,
so i do not inhale, merely hum
so low that no one hears but me;
under the clamor of our world, I hear the glamour of your voice,
still waiting to release the words you shoved down my gullet.

SCREAM!

people like to underestimate the power of sheer volume;
your silence accomplishes nothing.

I Kept My Integrity; Where's Yours?

You are your brother's keeper
You are your neighborhood watch
You are your family's pride
You are the goodwill of strangers.

We have a responsibility to uphold,
a collective secret to keep.
It only takes one to break the chain
Do not let go of my hand.

We are each other's safety.
We are each other's confidence.
We are our own aspirations.
We are the last resort.

You shall not choose who lives or who dies.
You shall rest in the power of the knowledge you have none.
We will be different than history has predicted.
We shall exercise the power of being fair.

My Mind Feels Like It Was Made for Losing

When the shades are drawn, there is a checkerboard of the northern lights
Ivory cream flowing in one ear and out the other,
Pupils oscillating under closed lids.
One thing streamlines into the next until I stand in a blur,
Comprehension is beyond me; understanding is disbelief.
Maybe this is what it feels like to lose one's mind.

Unyielding

If I said stop I don't want you here I don't want you near why are you talking so loud if my skin was my armor it is torn in places that I can never repair why won't you please stop talking stop talking I don't like the sound of your voice it is grating on my eardrums and pulling at my heartstrings please stop screaming a little bit of me breaks off every time you raise your voice another octave every time the music in your warble disappears you are stubborn I already know that but I already said to stop why do you keep going places where you are not wanted inserting yourself in situations where you are not allowed the sun sets and the stars rise and the earth spins on an axis but regardless of the time no matter the day you will... not... stop...

Cabin Fever

In Candyland looking through a sugar-glass window,
everything looks better than how it truly tastes;

acrid color and bitter shine.
So I will return to my window and let the door lock behind me.

Why Don't You Ever Listen?

You have always lived inside me
As a succubus inhabiting my chest cavity,
Sepsis slithering through my capillaries,
Taking my body under siege, my inescapable contagion.

I beg you to take flight before the succubus in my rib cage
Hooks her talons into the robust muscles of your back,
An unblemished utopia she thinks is perfect for razing.
I stand at a moral conundrum.

Now that we have sampled your splendor,
The roaring addiction begins.
What we call symbiotic, you call parasitic.
I will never let you go.

A Simple Thought:

I want to drown my reflection.

A Lovely Skeleton

The soft impressionist painting I have of you
In the inner corners of my mind
Makes a lovely skeleton
Lovelier than how you were to me.

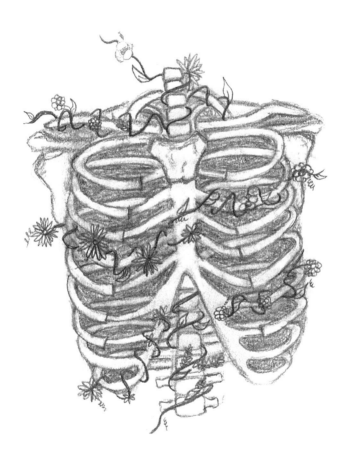

The Empress and the Fool

She is an ethereal flame captured in alabaster
She is power and dawning sunlight cascading down her back
She is of lithe limb and balmy temperament
Her voice the rivulet that will lead you to the ocean

He is brash, flamboyant
Young and undaunted
Light on his feet, and always dancing;
Irresistible charm that will only lead to trouble,

Teetering at the edge of a cliff,
Daring you to come stand with him.

An unlikely union to be sure
But together they feel like Strength,
A lion tamed by her soft hands,
Disciplined by his quick remarks.
Together they seem galactic.
They are life; they are bounty; they are eternal.

While his cup floweth over, hers is empty
She sees the bottom of what should have been bottomless
She can only give; he only takes.
Hands with the rough skin of a mother who works too much,
Kindness was mistaken for weakness

He gazes upon his reflection in the river of her voice,
Oblivious that he is looking into a dry bed
So she gives him a nudge and lets him fall into his oblivion;
He was already on the edge

The gold in her hair has grayed,

Her hell has frozen over

And so she bathes in the ash from her last fire,

Picks up a walking stick

And holds her lantern high above her head as she starts her trek into the dark.

when we close our eyes

when was i carried to sleep
to stop believing in Santa Claus,
which morning did i wake, telling myself
magic did not exist, the world was purely mortal
on what day did i decide that i was too grown up
to live my life in a fairytale,
flushed tulle and puffed sleeves

last year, playing dress up meant putting all my hair in a
baseball cap,
concealing instead of cultivating.
last march playing pretend was creating a racially ambiguous
persona,
productions that took the place of the cotton candy world I
grew up in;
the tufts of sugar are melting in my palms
slowly, with my pride,
collecting with prolific outrage.

when did we close our eyes and open them to a world of abhorrence
dictated by delusion, ruled by unease
why is it that, every time we open them again, it is all the same
twelve months later, and i am in stuck in the same fear,
tacky globs of rotting saccharine sugar still hanging off my frame,
the same sickness plaguing my stomach,
a familiar tempest fueling the fire in my belly.

A Two-Person Job

You inquire what you can do to lessen my load,
Question the pain that I carry,
Offering to neutralize the venom in my saliva

Weary of the choppy corners and jagged edges
Despite the faded incisions on your knuckles,
You nudge; I shove back.

You embrace me; and I wail
Encompassed by you, I should feel
Like I am in the safest place in the world

But I am still the mist that disappears every dawn,
A conscience still asking about a fork in the road
My life comes down to a series of split seconds

Decide now.

The time right now that is supposed to be mine
Is not mine at all,
Slipping through my fingers, puddling

Right next to the tears you cried
For every time I took a step
When you warned me I would fall.

Shelter

You are in the keys of my piano and the strings of my guitar.
You are every tremor,
The tone that rings in my ears,
The song in my head.

At times I see your mask on my wall,
Charred into the shadows cast by sunken cheeks.
Your fingers shape the roof over my head.
Skin the walls in which I burrow.

I exist in the spaces beneath your nails and the follicles of your hair.
I am an incantation and the source of your trepidation.
I make my home in the cones of your eyes.
Please do not forget me.

disappointment

I have every line of your face memorized your every curve all of the places that are impenetrable that only I can see stuck in a trance of swimming in your eyes and the condensation of the air you expunge but every time I look at every line I have memorized my faith drops down down down through the ebony earth I stand upon my toes curl reminding me that you will always disappoint me you will always fall short you will always fail in some way and no matter how many lines I trace with my lips i cannot stop you from the disillusion you will cause and the sting you leave behind.

When I'm Gone

The hour will come where I dissolve into particles rising to
the clouds,
Where I will mix with the same air that filled your swelling
chest
I will be in every sunrise, every crackle of the car stereo
I will still be there even when I'm gone.

Your memory will never fail you, regardless of the ardent ache
to forget
But if I am still the photograph in your wallet, how will you
undo your impotence
My perfume will be branded into your nostrils;
maybe everything will taste like that when I'm gone.

My figure is still in your door; my smile imprinted in your thoughts
Every lit candle will smell like we used to
Your car will want to take you back to where we met.
I know you'll still miss me even when I'm gone.

You will hear me murmur under every melody,

feel my touch every time you wake

Forever would never have been long enough

Still I slipped through your fingers, and now I'm gone.

These Are Just Words

Reputation bound to my ankles in shackles,
Weight.
Pulling down my shoulders until I cannot stand,
Baggage.
Enough to fill the belly of an airplane.
But I do promise,
And I give you my word
That no one will see you the way I do.
No one will marvel at your muddled charm and disheveled responses
No one can simultaneously adore and forgive all your mistakes
I crave to be inundated by pools of your daydreams
And I gave you my word,
The same you have heard before
Mine was the heart that knew how to love yours the best.

The Color Green

I would like to catch your voice in a jar,
Watch the colors twist and reform,
Sweet jade timbre and rippling satin
I say that as if it is as easy
As catching fireflies.

Fever Dreams

I am boiling from the inside out,
Quivering like a newborn butterfly,
Thirsting for this inferno to end.

If dreaming of you means
That you are thinking of me,
Then I should be in every dream you have.

I wake up drenched in my own sweat,
Conversing with a specter bearing an uncanny resemblance to you
But still cold, still shaking, still in pain.

The relief I begged for when the fever broke never came.
If I may only be with you in a spinning hell of a fever dream,
then I pray that my sickness never heals.

premature

there wasn't enough time to say goodbye to the place I called
home
i could not bid farewell to the womb where I began,
ripped out before I was ready to say goodbye
the outside is colder than I thought it would be
the solitude is drearier than you made it out to seem
sterile fluorescence blinds what little sight I have left
if I do not look then I can pretend that I am still in the home
that is you.

Hallowed Ground

You turned a two-lane highway into holy ground
and a barn into a castle,
dying trees into contentment,
small gestures to diamonds.

This will be immobilized in my memory
as the place where we first met for the second time,
where the gnarled tension in my stomach finally gave out
to make way for you to walk my house of mirrors.

Walk through the labyrinth with me,
where we will meet our fate at the center together.
Every turn you took is sacrosanct; we put on our paper crowns.
Remember, this is only goodbye for now.

Author's Note and Acknowledgments

I interviewed three people to glean a perspective on life that differs from my own. The following pieces are inspired by the extraordinary lives of Hafeeza S., Adam A., and everyone who took the time to speak with me. Thank you for your courage in sharing your stories.

heights

what is it about standing at the edge of something large that makes you feel so small your stomach tells you you are falling falling though your feet are still glued to the ground and your palms are beginning to sweat the ground swells beneath you and you are small so much so that you could be a speck a blip and then maybe you wouldn't be able to feel the impact when you hit the dirt because that is inevitable is it not it will come it is coming and so you close your eyes and find yourself rolling off the side of your bed

Puzzle Pieces

Steady hands, even breaths, balanced heartbeats—
painstakingly putting things back together, one microscopic
piece at a time.
Splinters stick out from the curves of your fingerprints;
the puzzle you are putting together is tinged with crusted red.

Shaky hands, shallow breaths, panicked heartbeats—
you cannot break what is already broken.
How do you watch someone you love tear the same thing apart
over and over and over again?
You've built your one-way mirror; now all you can do is watch.

A Lover of Language

Melted butter, letters, and gravy words slide down your throat.
You drink them in, forgetting that you cannot be heard.

You ask for more, swallow gulps of thick verse and gentle yarn.
You will learn to use them yet.

Alpha Female

You have pulled away from the pack as a pup and traveled miles.
Minuscule paws and soft toepads cut by the rocks and sore
from the distance—
they harden quickly; you hardly remember they are there.

You have breathed the thinning air and let your head spin
around the wind
when you have been to the mountaintop standing at the apex,
young eyes not quite yet understanding what they see,

young eyes drinking in the mesmeric lights fluttering across irises,
swallowing the promises the land has given you.
You consume it whole; it rests in your stomach

until you grow up; you bear children,
the promises you swallowed birthing themselves with them
sitting atop soft skulls. You saw the crown of their heads and you already knew.

"True peace is not merely the absence of tension; it is the presence of justice."
Your mother's cotton in your back pockets and your pen in your right hand, the almighty
clearing a path through every clouded judgement, deluded comment, unjust action—

no longer the same pup who carefully made her way up to the mountaintop.
Foot pads leathered and weathered by the years of picking up loose ends and throwing them
back in the faces of the people who dropped them and, without a glance back,

you throw your body over the weak, the lost, the unfortunate,
letting the blows ricochet off your hardened forepaws,
pushing, pushing towards the rainbow lights you swallowed,

fingers crawling down your throat to find them.
All the while, you scream for justice. The pack heeds your call;
they follow tiny prints to the mountaintop to say they have
been there too—

a road less travelled by—the one no one likes to talk about,

motherhood; battlefield,
sticks and stones and bones and shields,

funny looks, ungodly thoughts
ignorance and sentience naught.

break stiff molds, ace sticky tests,
battle the storm and give your children the best.

cold, long nights and worn-out shoes
a hate crime is a hate crime; a noose is still a noose.

Leading the Blind

Injustice to one becomes an injustice to all.

Only once we concede to the harsh reality of the truth will things get better.

You do everything in your power to help them see.

Imposter Syndrome

What do you do with a pretty face that has lost its voice?
When you feel like an imposter in your home, a stranger in
your bed?
There are disconnected screams to be acknowledged, yet
even when you meet it head to head, you find
you merely see yourself.
"*Exotic!*"
Mouth moving, speaking in a language you don't yet understand.

Ventilators

Reach one hand to the future, one to the past.
When you straddle the line between life and death,
gasping breaths and a silent mind,
utterly alone,
what else is there to do
but to grieve for the people who are hanging by the same thread
you were able to spin into a rope

Ostentation

There is a land full of peacocks and macaws that eat the livers of smaller birds.

Brown feathers arouse suspicion; what is divergent will not be celebrated.

The polychromatic flock pecks at your tail feathers.

What are you hiding from their rainbow feathers and staccato trills?

Hold your hatchlings close, their soft-bellied brown lining;

no matter how exceptioSnal their song, will always be a protrusion.

Made in the USA
Las Vegas, NV
07 February 2022

43379611R10069